THE BLACK BAPTIST PREACHER

THE BLACK BAPTIST PREACHER

HOW EFFECTIVE IS HIS THEOLOGY?

REV. SANFORD CHISOLM

XULON PRESS

Xulon Press
2301 Lucien Way #415
Maitland, FL 32751
407.339.4217
www.xulonpress.com

© 2019 by Rev. Sanford Chisolm

All rights reserved solely by the author. The author guarantees all contents are original and do not infringe upon the legal rights of any other person or work. No part of this book may be reproduced in any form without the permission of the author. The views expressed in this book are not necessarily those of the publisher.

Scripture taken from the New King James Version®. Copyright © 1982 by Thomas Nelson. Used by permission. All rights reserved.

Printed in the United States of America.

ISBN-13: 978-1-5456-7318-8

CONTENTS

Introduction ix
Chapter One   In the Beginning 1
Chapter Two   The Great Discovery 3
Chapter Three   His Divine Calling 5
Chapter Four   Respected Leader in His Community 7
Chapter Five   The Masters of Storytelling
                          in This Culture 11
Chapter Six   The Effectiveness of His Theology 13
Chapter Seven   The Black Baptist Preacher and His Journey
                          Towards Holiness 17

DEDICATION

I dedicate this book to my amazing family who supported me throughout all my endeavors; to my home church, Rodman Street Missionary Baptist Church, located in the East Liberty section of Pittsburgh, PA..to all of God's ministers who participated in this Preaching Ministry and have learned the awesome responsibility of becoming a Baptist Preacher. To Pastor/Prophet William Moody of Elisha Ministry Church, who was first to encourage me to exercise the gift that God has placed within me for the edifying of His Kingdom. Finally, to our beloved Pastor, Rev. Dr. Darryl T. Canady who epitomizes "The Black Baptist Preacher."

INTRODUCTION

My zeal for writing this revelatory book, came out of a special research project while attending The Reformed Presbyterian Theological Seminary. I decided to explore my deep conviction of how and why **The Black Baptist Preacher** became the forerunner of our Black Religious Traditions, impacting our culture from the depths of slavery to the heights of our personal religious freedom.

- Chapter One -

IN THE BEGINNING

The intriguing dynamics of Black History has always peaked my interest. Especially now that I have indulged my appetite into the selected readings of these famed Black Authors, such as Franklin, Harding, Roboteau, Wilmore, and Fitts, just to name a few. I'm most appreciative of the selection made by Professor L.J. Walker, to use John H. Franklin and Alfred A. Moss, Jr's. book, "From Slavery To Freedom," as a course study, for our dramatic, exciting, authoritative story of the experiences of African Americans from the time they left the shores of Africa, to their continued struggle for equality at the end of the twentieth century.

Now that I have satisfied my curiosty, somewhat, in regard to African American Church History and Polity, its impact on African American Culture in the past, present and future, I am ready to focus on the title of my book; The Black Baptist Preacher. Also, I want to explore as my sub-title, "How Effective Is His Theology?" In reading the book by Leroy Fitts, "A History Of Black Baptists," I discovered that the information contained in his book was exactly where I wanted to start my quest on The Black Baptist Preacher. Who was he? How did he learn to do what he does? According to

L. Fitts "Long before the clash between white Baptists over the issue of slavery, there were some black Baptist leaders who gradually became aware of the need of separate churches from whites."

- Chapter Two -
THE GREAT DISCOVERY

It's my understanding that the Black Preacher emerged from the "ashes" of the separation of white and black Baptist leaders, therefore forming what they called Plantation Missions. It was at these missions that the white plantation owners discovered that the Black Preacher had the gift to preach God's Word. The plantation owner was so impressed that he granted him "privilege papers" to preach anywhere on their plantations. When its time for God's Word to get through to His people, God will make a way out of no way. The secret meetings that these preachers had in the middle of the night, time after time, finally through the power of God's Word, reached the masses. The Bible teaches us in Philippians 4:6-7 "To be anxious for nothing; but in everything by prayer and supplication with thanksgiving, let your requests be made known unto God. And the peace of God, which passes all understanding, shall keep your hearts and minds through Christ Jesus." I know these Black Preachers were not privy to reading God's Word from the Bible like their white counterpart, but I believe they had something better; the Holy Spirit was their teacher and He brought back to their remembrance the Word that they heard and they were able to preach that Word under the Anointing. Eventually, as the slaves were encourged by their black preachers, they grew in grace and knowledge of the Lord Jesus Christ. These preaching services and prayer meetings soon became the antecedents to organized Black Baptist Churches. The Black Baptist Preacher with the indwelling Spirit led him to preach. Many slaves in those days were converted and empowered to keep hope alive.

- Chapter Three -

HIS DIVINE CALLING

When I do a comparison of the Black Preacher today, especially in the Baptist denomination, the preacher becomes more than they are called to do. They preach and teach, they are sometimes called on to heal the sick, they are the community organizers, he or she is involved in politics, they are the marriage counselors, the divorce counselors; in other words, they are all that they can be through Christ Jesus who strengthens them. Black Baptist Preachers are great orators; their history goes back to the late 1700s. According to L. Fitts survey of Baptist beginnings in Georgia, "The First Colored Baptist Church, Savannah, Georgia, perhaps the oldest black Baptist church in America, was organized January 20, 1788, by Andrew Bryan along with a few slaves to whom he had preached the Gospel."

The power of hearing the gospel preached reminds me of when I was very young, being a member of the Second Baptist Church Of Blairsville, a small town in Indiana County, Pennsylvania; that preacher would preach a sermon that kept me wanting to do right for several weeks at a time. There was something about how he preached that Word of God that stayed in my mind. I believe that was when the seed of Faith was planted in my spirit. My mother used to tell me that one day I was going to become a Preacher. At sixteen years of age, I never gave those words any thought. Today, I'm proud to say that I answered the call of the Lord to preach His Word.

- Chapter Four -
RESPECTED LEADER IN HIS COMMUNITY

What kind of leader is the Black Baptist Preacher in his community? There are several Baptist Preachers who are so involved in politics that they hold political offices. I believe this new found freedom that has emerged in today's church could do more damage than good. God said that we are suppose to be in the world, but not of the world. Can it be that the Kingdom of God is expanding so rapidly that our Black Baptist Preacher is losing his way? I pray that this deception is uncovered before it affects the Church at large. Leadership should be second nature to the Black Baptist Preacher because he or she is a part of a legacy that stretches back to over three hundred years. We have had some very powerful leaders that came out of the black Baptist church. What was their agenda? Are they carrying out God's agenda for His people, or just being heads of Great Organazations? Some of us, who are waiting for the right answers, find ourselves caught up in the moment. In the moment of time when the church, the Body of Christ, is losing sight of God's agenda and implementing their own. The statistics are staggering in the battle for our souls in the church. Are we losing our very souls because the Word of God is being preached at the church and not to the church. Are we as a black church, waiting for our charismatic Black Baptist Preacher to re-emancipate us all over again? The Black Baptist Preacher was at his best when he was being oppressed. Now that freedom rings, prayers have been answered, is the battle over? Who can truly address what our soul needs? Jesus was the answer then and Jesus is the answer now!

I was really impressed with W.E. Burghardt DuBois; The Souls of Black Folk. I would like to quote a portion of his work, I found it to be soul searching. This is what he wrote; "It is difficult to explain clearly the present critical stage of Negro religion. First, we must remember that living as the blacks do in close contact with a great modern nation, and sharing, although imperfectly, the soul-life of that nation, they must necessarily be affected more or less directly by all the religious and ethical forces that are today moving the United States. These questions and movements are, however, overshadowed and dwarfed by the (to them) all-important question of their civil, political, and economic status."

The Black Baptist Preacher holds the key to the ever-evolving doors of the church. In times past we enjoyed the status of a great Baptist preacher named Rev. Dr. Martin Luther King. With his political connections and national status as being the spiritual leader of the black movement, his loss was devastating to our cause. Throughout his ministry, Dr. King preached the black story, along with the biblical story to rally his followers to keep the faith during their most difficult times. Here is an example of how he inspired the Montgomery, Alabama bus boycotters; "We are here this evening because we are tired now, but let us say that we are not here advocating violence. We have overcome that. I want it to be known throughout Montgomery and throughout this nation that we are a Christian people. We believe in Christian religion. We believe in the teachings of Jesus. The only weapon that we have in our hands this everning is the weapon of protest...This is the glory of America, with all of its faults...The great glory of American democracy is the right to protest for right." How exciting it was when we thought the Rev. Jesse Jackson could possibly be the replacement for the late Dr. Martin Luther King. He so graciously coined the phrase "Let's Keep Hope Alive." He ran for the Presidency of the United States. He had charisma and was very intelligent. For the moment, he represented his black people very well. After all, like Martin, Jesse was a Black Baptist Preacher. What can we say about our Black Baptist Preachers? They can provide the leadership needed to move a nation toward God. Can the two cultures come together for the sake of unifying the body of Christ? In the political arena, in the pulpit of the black churches, our Black Baptist Preachers have proven to be the answer to our nation's ills.

The Bible says that the wheat and tares will grow together until it is time for the harvest. At that time, the Lord himself will do the harvesting. What does that mean to the Black Baptist Preacher? Since this world and all its politics is temporary, all of us who claim to be preaching God's Word and carrying out His agenda, better get it right before our Lord returns.

There is one more Black Baptist Preacher I would like to bring to the table of Hope: The Rev. Al Sharpton. Can he deliver the Message of Hope to the Black nation? How about to the entire nation? Remember this nation, who at this moment is claiming to be living under the grace and mercy of God, advocating, neither black nor white. Praise the Lord, we have finally embraced the concept of diversity. I believe that the fate of our religiosity is in the hands of the Almighty God.

- Chapter Five -

THE MASTERS OF STORYTELLING IN THIS CULTURE

Words can create worlds. It has been said by some, that the Black Baptist Preacher, through the virtuosity of imaginative, lyrical, and poetic language, and the co-creativity of a responsive congregation, brings the sacred and human realms together. This is another one of Robert M. Franklin's quotes from his book, Another Day's Journey. "Black preachers may be responsible for keeping alive the great tradition of storytelling in American culture. They provide a narrative framework within which hearers can interpret public life in a compelling way. The narrative draws people in, inviting them to evaluate the moral hygiene of the state, market, and civil society. They use biblical categories and themes such as exodus, crucifixion, resurrection, sin, and redemption to help people think historically and critically about the condition of the community." The Black Baptist Preacher is a product of our great heritage and no other ethnic group can qualify to be his replacement. It is as if God Himself came down from Heaven one glorious night and declared to the congregation, "I am the Lord your God and you are my people, and I will lift you up at the appointed time." Could it be that in those back woods of a particular plantation, these religious slaves encountered a Divine visitation? Even though many of them could not read or write the language of their foreign land, I believe that they could recognize the presence of the Holy Spirit.

I agree with the writer of The Souls Of Black Folk, when W.E. Burghardt DuBois made this comment; "Three things characterized this religion of the slave, the Preacher, the Music, and the Frenzy. The Preacher is the most unique personality developed by the Negro on American soil. A leader, a politician, an orator, a boss, an intriguer, an idealist, all these he is, and ever, too, the center of a group of men, now twenty, now a thousand in number."

- Chapter Six -

THE EFFECTIVENESS OF HIS THEOLOGY

The sub title of my book, "How Effective Is His Theology?" I would like to explore this subject in terms of his effectiveness as a Black Baptist Preacher. It goes without saying, that God through His Son by the way of the Holy Spirit, made special provision for this man of God to effectively speak to his people. What this preacher knew about God was a result of him falling on his knees and asking God to come into his life and set him free from the bondage of slavery. At that very moment, I believe the process started. The scripture reminds us in the book of Hebrews 11:6, "But without faith it is impossible to please Him; for he that cometh to God must believe that He is, and that He is a rewarder of them that diligently seek Him." Again I remind you that these slaves were not privileged to have the Bible as we have today, to make reference to the scriptures. I believe that they were the products of the Word coming alive in their souls. The living Word verses the written Word. After all, their masters unknowingly exposed them to the written Word as they attended their church services.

Their particular setting kind of reminds me what it was like when I attended my first Greek class; the words were being spoken clearly to all of us, but I just didn't understand them. But before the semester was over, I was able to speak and understand the Greek language as it related to the Word of God. Remember this, when you are passionate about learning God's Word, He always gives you the victory so that He can get the glory! I believe that these early Baptist Preachers were passionate about learning God's Word and once they learned, they couldn't wait to steal away at one of their prayer meetings to share with their brethern. God always makes a way out of no way.

What does all of this have to do with Theology? What is Theology? Theology is the study of the nature of God and religious truth. Asking and probing rational religious questions. Some would even call Theology, a system or school of opinions concerning God and religious questions. Last but not least, a third definition of Theology is a course of specialized religious study usually at a college or seminary. Did the religious activities of the slaves bring them into the knowledge of the truth concerning the nature of God? I believe that their Theology was as real to them as it is to us today. They believed in the power of the Holy Spirit to teach them all that they needed to know about God. They believed that God answers Prayer. Even though in some cases it did not happen right away, they still believed. Gods' time is different from our time; His ways are higher than our ways. The Holy Spirit reveals the nature of God. God said in His Word, "He is no respecter of persons, what He has done for you, He will do for them." That is what is so wonderful about the nature of God, He condescends to where you are, because He is the Creator and we are His creatures. Based on my limited research, I'm sure that the masters of the plantation had no idea when they allowed the slaves to attend their church services, they would develop their own Spirit given Theology. Based on God's Sovereignty, everything happens according to His perfect will. Was it the will of God for these slaves to understand His nature? The Theology of the slaves was just as real to them as the Theology of the free men.

- Chapter Seven -

THE BLACK BAPTIST PREACHER AND HIS JOURNEY TOWARDS HOLINESS

The Black Baptist Preacher will always continue to study to show himself approved unto God, and be that workman who does not need to be ashamed and rightly divides the Word of Truth. I believe that he or she will always pursue our God in the various ways He allows us. None of us will learn it all. As a matter of fact, it is written in the scriptures, that we only know in part and when Jesus returns, all knowledge will be fulfilled in Him.

If we as Black Baptist Preachers are to continue on the path towards Holiness, we must remember that God has already told our story in His Word. He is the Alpha and the Omega, the beginning and the end.

As one who has been called to preach the Good news, which is the Gospel of the Lord Jesus the Christ, the infalible Word of the living God, allow me to share this awesome truth; If you don't seek the Anointing before you begin to preach, your preaching will be in vain. In other words, without the moving of the Holy Spirit, your preaching will lack the power to overcome the obstacles our enemy places in our way. Apostle Paul writes in his letter to the Ephesians, chapter 6:10, "Finally my brethern, be strong in the Lord and in the power of His might." What was he trying to warn the Black Baptist Preacher in today's world? Without the Holy Spirit, we are powerless against our enemy, Satan.

As Baptist Preachers, are we truly called by the Lord, to preach the message of Salvation? Listen to what Jesus says in scripture. The Bible records these words in Matthew 22:14, the story of the Wedding Feast; Jesus presents a parable to illustrate that many are called, but few are chosen. How do we as Baptist Preachers, know if we are among the few that have been chosen, or have ears to hear? By responding to the call, assurance of this certain call, the chosen call, is from the Holy Spirit. Look at what Apostle Paul says in Philippians 1:6, which says, "Being confident of this, that He who began a good work in you will carry it on to the completion until the day of Christ Jesus." If God has chosen you and you are available for His use, you must always preach under the Anointing. Without the Holy Spirit leading you down the path of Righteousness, you will lose your way.

To take on the awesome responsibility of preaching the Good news, you have to be willing to follow the protocol that our Baptist forerunners set in motion; The power of prayer! What holds true when God spoke to the Saints of old, in II Chronicles 7:14, holds true to this day. "If my people which are called by my name, shall humble themselves, and pray, and seek my face, and turn from their wicked ways, then will I hear from heaven, and will forgive their sin, and will heal their land."

I prayerfully recommend that we as Black Baptist Preachers, continue to pursue formal theological education so that we can be more effective in our ministries. A high percentage of the African American clergy lacks formal theological education. So that I will not be judged by others as being hypocritical, I will always believe that if we are being oppressed in any way and we have been chosen to serve our God ,He will intervene and give us what we need to carry out His will for His people. As a final thought, If you have any doubt, while you are pressing toward the mark of your high calling, seek the Anointing.

www.ingramcontent.com/pod-product-compliance
Ingram Content Group UK Ltd.
Pitfield, Milton Keynes, MK11 3LW, UK
UKHW022217230426
12048UKWH00016BA/909